Financial Freedom: Navigating the Wealth of Knowledge

Introduction to Personal Finance

Personal finance is a term that encompasses the management of an individual's financial resources. It involves making informed decisions about earning, spending, saving, and investing money to achieve financial goals and security. In this chapter, we will delve into the foundational concepts of personal finance, its significance, its historical evolution, how this book is structured, and the learning objectives you can expect to achieve.

Definition of Personal Finance

Personal finance, as the name suggests, is about managing your money on a personal level. It involves making decisions about how you earn, spend, save, and invest your income. It encompasses a wide range of financial activities, from budgeting and saving to investing for the future and planning for retirement. In essence, personal finance is the process of making your money work for you and achieving your financial aspirations.

The Importance of Financial Management

Financial management is a critical aspect of personal finance. It involves the art of budgeting, saving, and investing wisely to ensure that your financial present and future are secure. Proper financial management helps individuals avoid debt, build wealth, and prepare for unexpected expenses or emergencies. It also enables individuals to pursue their life goals and dreams with financial confidence.

A Brief History of Personal Finance

The concept of personal finance has evolved over time. In the past, financial management was often learned through experience or passed down from one generation to another. It wasn't until the 20th century that personal finance education became more widespread. The Great Depression in the 1930s and the subsequent economic changes emphasized the importance of financial literacy. Today, personal finance education is readily available through schools, books, online resources, and financial advisors.

How This Book Works

This book is designed to be your comprehensive guide to personal finance. It will cover various aspects of managing your finances, from budgeting and saving to investing and planning for retirement. Each chapter is dedicated to a specific topic and is packed with practical advice, examples, and strategies to help you make informed financial decisions.

Learning Objectives

By the end of this book, you will have a solid understanding of the following key personal finance concepts:

1. The fundamentals of personal finance and the role it plays in your life.
2. How to create a budget and track your expenses effectively.
3. The importance of saving money and how to build an emergency fund.
4. Strategies for managing and reducing debt.
5. How to maintain a good credit score and manage credit wisely.
6. The basics of insurance and how to select the right policies for your needs.
7. Introduction to various types of investments and their risk and return profiles.
8. Retirement planning, including pension funds and individual retirement accounts.
9. The impact of taxation on your financial planning.

10.	Estate planning and the importance of wills.
11.	Strategies for achieving financial independence and early retirement.
12.	Sustainable and ethical investing for aligning your values with your investment choices.

Setting Financial Goals

In the vast and complex world of personal finance, establishing clear and well-defined financial objectives serves as the compass guiding individuals toward a future of financial stability and prosperity. This chapter delves into the foundational principles of financial goal setting. We will explore the profound importance of these objectives, distinguish between short-term, mid-term, and long-term financial goals, uncover the concept of SMART goals (Specific, Measurable, Achievable, Realistic, and Time-bound), and discuss the continual process of monitoring and updating your financial aspirations.

The Significance of Financial Goals

Financial goals are the bedrock of an effective financial plan. They provide a sense of purpose, motivation, and a clear sense of direction in the realm of personal finance. Without well-defined financial targets, it's easy to drift aimlessly through life, making financial decisions without a clear destination in mind. Setting financial goals is the powerful first step in seizing control of your financial destiny and ensuring that your earnings are purposefully channeled toward achieving the life you envision.

Financial goals offer a multitude of advantages:

1. **Focus and Clarity**: By setting clear goals, you can discern precisely what you wish to accomplish and prioritize your financial decisions accordingly.
2. **Motivation**: Goals serve as the impetus for saving, investing, and making sound financial choices. They give you a reason to strive for financial growth.
3. **Progress Evaluation**: Specific objectives allow you to gauge your financial progress. They offer you the opportunity to adapt and refine your strategy if necessary.

Short-Term, Mid-Term, and Long-Term Goals

Financial goals come in various shapes and sizes, and categorizing them based on their time horizon is crucial. Goals can generally be classified into three broad categories: short-term, mid-term, and long-term.

- **Short-term goals**, as the name suggests, encompass objectives that can be achieved in the near future, usually within a year or less. These may include building an emergency fund, paying off high-interest credit card debt, or saving for an upcoming vacation.

- **Mid-term goals** extend beyond the immediate future, typically covering a time frame of one to five years. Such goals may encompass saving for a down payment on a home, funding a child's education, or upgrading to a newer car.
- **Long-term goals** are ambitions that span five years or more. They often pertain to retirement planning, purchasing a home, or achieving financial independence.

Balancing these different types of goals is paramount as it ensures that you are addressing your various financial needs and aspirations in a holistic manner.

Creating SMART Goals

Setting financial goals is a powerful endeavor, but it's only truly effective when those goals are SMART—Specific, Measurable, Achievable, Realistic, and Time-bound.

1. **Specific**: Your goal should be clear and well-defined. Instead of stating a vague aspiration like, "I want to save money," consider a more precise goal such as, "I want to save $10,000 for a down payment on a home."
2. **Measurable**: Effective goals should be quantifiable. This means you should be able to track your progress. For example, a measurable goal could involve reducing your credit card debt by $5,000 within a year.

3. **Achievable**: Your goal should be realistic and within reach. While it's admirable to aim high, it's equally important to ensure your goals are attainable based on your current financial circumstances.
4. **Realistic**: Your goals should be grounded in your life and financial situation. It's crucial that your goals are both realistic and in alignment with your values and priorities.
5. **Time-bound**: Every goal needs a deadline. Establishing a specific time frame adds a sense of urgency and encourages consistent effort. For instance, you might aspire to save $15,000 for a family vacation within three years.

Monitoring and Updating Goals

The process of setting financial goals is not a one-time event; it's an ongoing journey. Life is dynamic, and as circumstances evolve, so should your financial aspirations. Regularly monitoring your progress is vital. It enables you to assess whether you are on track and whether adjustments are needed.

Flexibility is key when it comes to financial goal setting. Unforeseen financial challenges or opportunities may arise, necessitating adjustments to your objectives. The crucial point is to stay committed to your financial well-being and be adaptable in your quest for a more secure and fulfilling financial future.

Budgeting and Tracking Expenses

Budgeting, often regarded as the bedrock of sound personal finance, is the art of allocating your financial resources strategically, ensuring that your income is effectively directed toward meeting your needs, achieving your financial goals, and securing your future. This chapter delves into the multifaceted world of budgeting and explores the pivotal practice of tracking expenses. Here, we aim to provide you with comprehensive insights into how to create a budget, understand the dynamics of your income and expenditures, and discern areas where you can enhance your financial well-being by saving money effectively.

The Role of Budgeting

Budgeting is an indispensable process that serves as a financial roadmap for individuals and households. Its importance extends far beyond the simple allocation of resources; it encapsulates the very essence of responsible financial stewardship. Here's why budgeting plays such a critical role:

1. **Gaining Clarity**: A budget offers you unparalleled clarity about your financial life. It's akin to illuminating a dark room; it exposes where your money originates and how it flows through your life.

2. **Setting Priorities**: With a budget, you possess the ability to prioritize your financial objectives. You can make informed decisions about where to allocate your limited financial resources.

3. **Tracking Progress**: Budgets provide an ongoing mechanism for tracking your financial progress. They serve as a yardstick against which you can measure your accomplishments and recalibrate your strategy as needed.

4. **Avoiding Overspending**: An effective budget acts as a safety net, preventing reckless spending and protecting you from accumulating debt.

Creating Your Budget

The creation of a budget involves a sequence of essential steps, each contributing to the overall efficacy of your financial plan:

1. **Determining Your Income**: Initiate the budgeting process by calculating your total monthly income. This includes your regular salary, any supplementary income from side gigs or investments, rental income, and all other sources of revenue that contribute to your financial inflow.

2. **Listing Your Expenses**: Compile an exhaustive list of your monthly expenses, categorizing them into two primary segments: fixed and variable expenditures. Fixed expenses comprise recurring financial obligations such as mortgage or rent payments, utilities, and insurance premiums. Variable expenses, on the other hand, encompass the more flexible aspects of your budget, including groceries, dining out, entertainment, and miscellaneous discretionary spending.

3. **Setting Financial Goals**: Identifying your financial goals, both short-term and long-term, is pivotal to effective budgeting. Whether your goals involve paying off debt, amassing funds for an upcoming vacation, building an emergency fund, or pursuing a long-term investment strategy, your budget serves as the vehicle to reach those milestones.

4. **Creating Your Budget**: Armed with an understanding of your income and expenses, you can proceed to establish your budget. This can be executed through various tools, from dedicated budgeting software and apps to manual methods involving spreadsheets. In essence, your budget allots specific amounts to each expenditure category, with the overarching rule that your total expenses must not surpass your total income.

5. **Regular Review and Adjustment**: A static budget is rarely effective over the long term. Life is characterized by dynamic change, and your financial plan must adapt accordingly. Regularly review your budget to ensure it remains in line with your financial aspirations and life circumstances. Should unexpected changes occur, be prepared to make adjustments.

The Importance of Tracking Expenses

Integral to the budgeting process is the practice of tracking expenses. This entails meticulous documentation of every financial outlay, providing a granular perspective on where your money is expended. Here are some of the reasons why expense tracking is fundamental:

1. **Identification of Spending Patterns**: Expense tracking unveils your spending habits. It is akin to having a financial mirror that reflects your daily choices. By understanding your financial behaviors, you can take conscious steps to manage your money more effectively.
2. **Prevention of Overspending**: A well-executed expense tracking system operates as a financial conscience. It discourages impulsive or excessive spending, as the act of recording each expense fosters mindfulness regarding your financial limits.
3. **Staying On Budget**: Expense tracking ensures that your actual spending aligns with your budget. By comparing your recorded expenses to your budget, you can pinpoint areas where you may be exceeding your allocated limits and make necessary adjustments.

Budgeting Tools and Strategies

A variety of tools and strategies exist to facilitate effective budgeting and expense tracking:

1. **Envelope System**: This time-tested method involves the allocation of cash into envelopes, each designated for specific spending categories such as groceries, entertainment, or dining out. When the cash within a particular envelope is depleted, spending in that category ceases for the remainder of the month.
2. **Budgeting Apps**: In the digital age, an array of budgeting apps have emerged to simplify the process. Software such as Mint, YNAB (You Need A Budget), and Personal Capital can automate expense tracking and budgeting, providing real-time insights into your financial health.
3. **Spreadsheet Software**: Many individuals opt for the flexibility of creating their budget in spreadsheet software like Microsoft Excel or Google Sheets. This approach enables high customization and detailed expense tracking.
4. **Cash Flow Statement**: A cash flow statement is a comprehensive overview of your income and expenses, revealing the dynamics of your financial life. By creating a cash flow statement, you can gain a holistic perspective on your financial situation.

5. **Periodic Reviews**: Your budget is not a static document; it is a dynamic tool that should be subject to regular review. Periodic assessment of your expenses allows you to make data-driven decisions, renegotiate service contracts, find more affordable alternatives, and eliminate unnecessary expenses.

Overcoming Common Budgeting Challenges

Budgeting can present challenges, and it's important to address these proactively. Some common hurdles to successful budgeting include:

1. **Emergency Fund**: Maintain an emergency fund as part of your financial safety net to cover unforeseen expenses without disrupting your budget. These savings provide peace of mind and financial security.

2. **Savings for Irregular Expenses**: Irregular expenses, such as vacations, holiday gifts, or annual insurance premiums, should be anticipated and budgeted for. Allocate a small portion of your budget each month to fund these irregular but expected costs.

3. **Consistent Tracking**: To ensure that expense tracking remains effective, make it a habit to document your expenditures consistently. Depending on your preference, this can be done daily, weekly, or at another regular interval. Consistency leads to accurate data and informed decisions.

4. **Variable Income**: If your income fluctuates due to irregular paychecks, freelance work, or variable commissions, create a budget based on your lowest expected monthly income. Use windfalls, bonuses, or extra income to enhance savings or accelerate debt reduction.

5. **Lifestyle Adjustments**: Be prepared to adjust your lifestyle as necessary to adhere to your budget. Evaluate and prioritize your expenses to align with your financial goals. This may involve eliminating or reducing expenses that no longer align with your priorities.

In conclusion, budgeting and tracking expenses are integral components of sound financial management. They offer you the means to take control of your financial life, reduce financial stress, and make well-informed decisions about your money.

Building an Emergency Fund and Managing Debt

In the intricate realm of personal finance, two foundational pillars emerge as essential components of financial stability: the establishment of an emergency fund and the prudent management of debt. This chapter is dedicated to exploring the significance of an emergency fund and providing insights and strategies for the responsible management of debt. By the end of this chapter, you'll have a comprehensive understanding of how to safeguard your financial well-being by preparing for unexpected expenses and handling debt effectively.

Section 1: Building an Emergency Fund

An emergency fund serves as a financial safety net, designed to provide protection when unexpected financial challenges arise. Let's delve into the critical aspects of creating and maintaining this essential financial cushion.

The Importance of an Emergency Fund

Financial emergencies can strike at any time, whether it's a medical expense, car repair, or an unforeseen job loss. An emergency fund offers financial security and peace of mind, serving as a means to prevent accumulating high-interest debt when confronted with unexpected expenses.

How Much to Save

The ideal size of your emergency fund varies based on individual circumstances. A common guideline suggests aiming for three to six months' worth of living expenses. However, factors such as job stability, family size, and existing financial commitments should be considered in determining the appropriate amount.

Building Your Emergency Fund

To build your emergency fund, set a savings target, automate contributions, cut unnecessary expenses, and use windfalls or unexpected financial gains to accelerate your progress.

Where to Keep Your Emergency Fund

Your emergency fund should be easily accessible, but not so readily accessible that it tempts you for non-emergencies. Consider options like a high-yield savings account or a money market account for the right balance of accessibility and higher interest rates.

Section 2: Managing Debt

Debt is a common financial reality, but effective debt management is key to maintaining financial health. This section provides insights into managing and eventually eliminating debt.

Understanding Different Types of Debt

Debt can be categorized into two primary types: good debt, which can potentially contribute to wealth-building, and bad debt, which typically does not generate wealth and can become financially burdensome.

The Impact of Debt on Your Finances

Debt can affect your financial health in several ways, from accruing interest costs to impacting your credit score and reducing your ability to save and invest for the future.

Creating a Debt Repayment Plan

Effectively managing debt involves creating a structured plan:

- Listing Your Debts: Start by documenting all your outstanding debts, including the current balance, interest rate, and minimum payment for each debt.
- Prioritizing High-Interest Debt: Focus on paying down debts with the highest interest rates first, as this minimizes the overall interest costs incurred.

- Snowball vs. Avalanche Method: Two widely adopted strategies for debt repayment are the debt snowball method and the debt avalanche method. In the former, you concentrate on paying off the smallest debt first, gaining a psychological boost and building momentum. The latter strategy targets debts with the highest interest rates, minimizing the long-term cost of borrowing.
- Budget for Debt Repayment: Allocate a specific portion of your budget for debt repayment. This dedicated allocation ensures that you make consistent progress in reducing your debt load.

Avoiding New Debt

While diligently repaying existing debt, it is crucial to avoid accumulating new debt, as this ensures that your debt management efforts remain effective:

- Budgeting: Maintain a well-structured budget that aligns with your financial goals, ensuring that you live within your means and do not incur further debt.
- Emergency Fund: Your emergency fund, as discussed earlier, serves as a financial safety net. With an adequate fund in place, you are less likely to accumulate new debt when unexpected expenses arise.

- Credit Card Management: Wisely manage your credit cards by paying off balances in full each month to avoid interest charges and the accrual of credit card debt.

Section 3: Case Study - Jane's Journey

A case study of Jane, a fictional character, offers a real-world narrative that illustrates how to build an emergency fund and manage debt in a practical context. By delving into Jane's experiences, this section provides practical insights and strategies that can be applied to your own financial journey.

Section 4: Tips and Strategies

This section provides a range of practical tips and strategies for building an emergency fund and effectively managing debt. These encompass:

- Balancing Debt and Savings: Striking the right balance between debt repayment and savings, tailored to your unique circumstances, ensures holistic financial well-being.
- Negotiating with Creditors: In the face of financial hardship, do not hesitate to engage with creditors to negotiate temporary relief, which can help you navigate challenging times.

- **Emergency Fund Refill:** After using your emergency fund for its intended purpose, prioritize replenishing it as soon as possible. A fully funded emergency fund is the linchpin of your financial security.
- **Lifestyle Adjustments:** Consider making adjustments to your lifestyle to free up additional funds for savings and debt repayment. Sometimes, small changes can lead to significant financial improvements.
- **Financial Counseling:** If the management of debt becomes overwhelming or unmanageable, it is advisable to seek the guidance of a financial counselor or advisor who can provide specialized assistance and strategies.

Saving and Investing for Your Future

In the multifaceted landscape of personal finance, the realms of saving and investing emerge as twin titans, pivotal in shaping your financial well-being and securing your future. This chapter delves into the intricate fabric of saving and investing, unraveling the core principles, strategies, and the significance these actions hold in achieving your financial goals.

The Power of Saving

Saving, at its core, embodies the act of setting aside a portion of your income for future use. It's more than a financial practice; it's a disciplined commitment to securing your financial well-being and achieving your aspirations. At the heart of saving lies the fundamental principle of responsible financial management.

Understanding the Fundamentals of Saving

To begin our journey into the world of saving, it's essential to understand the fundamentals. Saving transcends mere monetary actions; it embodies a mindset, a way of life. The saving habit entails consistent dedication to putting a portion of your income towards your financial goals. This practice should be ingrained in your lifestyle, not seen as a mere option.

The Importance of an Emergency Fund

A cornerstone of saving is the establishment of an emergency fund. The role of an emergency fund is paramount, providing a financial safety net when unexpected challenges arise. It serves as a bulwark against financial crises, ensuring that you can navigate unforeseen expenses without resorting to high-interest loans or credit cards.

Short-Term vs. Long-Term Saving

Distinguishing between short-term and long-term saving is pivotal for effective financial planning. Short-term saving caters to goals you intend to achieve within the next few years, such as a vacation, a down payment for a car, or home appliances. These goals often necessitate readily accessible funds. In contrast, long-term saving focuses on objectives further in the future, such as retirement or purchasing a home. The extended time horizon for these goals enables a different approach to investment.

The World of Investing

While saving acts as the foundation of financial stability, investing serves as the engine for wealth accumulation. It's the mechanism through which your financial resources can grow over time. In an ever-changing economic landscape, the role of investing becomes increasingly significant.

The Case for Investing

Investing is more than a financial choice; it's a financial imperative. Its significance lies in its potential to outpace the eroding effects of inflation. Inflation diminishes the purchasing power of your money over time, making it vital to place your funds where they can grow.

Diverse Investment Vehicles and Options

The world of investing is vast, offering a diverse array of vehicles and options, each with its unique characteristics, risk profiles, and potential returns. These encompass stocks, bonds, mutual funds, exchange-traded funds (ETFs), real estate, retirement accounts, savings accounts, certificates of deposit (CDs), and even alternative investments such as commodities and private equity. Each investment vehicle serves a specific purpose and risk tolerance.

Risk, Diversification, and Setting Goals

Understanding the complex landscape of investing involves comprehending the inherent risks, embracing diversification, and setting clear financial goals.

Understanding Risk

Risk is an integral part of investing. It comes in various forms, including market risk, credit risk, and liquidity risk. Market risk pertains to the chance that the overall market may decline, affecting the value of your investments. Credit risk is associated with the likelihood that issuers of debt instruments may fail to make interest payments or repay the principal. Liquidity risk involves the possibility that you may not be able to sell an investment at your desired price due to a lack of buyers.

The Role of Diversification

Diversification is a potent risk management strategy. It involves spreading your investments across different asset classes, industries, and geographic regions to reduce the impact of adverse events on your portfolio. By diversifying, you minimize the risk associated with putting all your resources into a single investment.

Setting Clear Financial Goals

Investing should be guided by clear financial goals. These objectives serve as the North Star, directing your investment strategy. Financial goals should be specific, measurable, achievable, relevant, and time-bound (SMART). They provide the roadmap that shapes your investment portfolio and helps you stay on course.

In conclusion, the synergy of saving and investing is the cornerstone of securing your financial future. While saving is the foundation, investing acts as the engine that propels your financial resources toward growth. As you delve into the intricate world of investing, it's essential to grasp the nuances of risk, the advantages of diversification, and the power of setting clear financial goals.

Retirement Planning and Wealth Accumulation

In the intricate tapestry of personal finance, retirement planning emerges as one of the most significant and transformative phases of your financial journey. This chapter explores the multifaceted world of retirement planning, guiding you through the critical aspects of building a secure retirement, wealth accumulation, and strategies to ensure financial well-being in your golden years.

The Essence of Retirement Planning

Retirement, often viewed as the crowning chapter of one's life, represents a time when the fruits of a lifetime of labor can be enjoyed to the fullest. To embark on this journey with confidence, meticulous retirement planning is essential. It involves setting financial goals, assessing your current financial position, and developing a comprehensive strategy to achieve those goals.

The Importance of Setting Clear Retirement Goals

The very foundation of retirement planning is setting clear and realistic goals. These goals encompass both financial and lifestyle aspirations. Whether it's traveling the world, pursuing a passion, or simply enjoying a peaceful retirement, having well-defined objectives is essential to ensure your financial plan aligns with your vision for retirement.

Assessing Your Current Financial Position

A thorough assessment of your current financial situation is the next critical step. This involves evaluating your assets, including savings, investments, and any other potential income streams. Simultaneously, a comprehensive analysis of your liabilities, such as outstanding debts or financial commitments, is imperative to ascertain your net worth. Understanding your financial position provides a baseline from which your retirement plan can take shape.

The Role of Social Security and Pension Plans

Social Security and employer-sponsored pension plans can play a significant role in your retirement income. It's essential to understand the benefits you'll receive from these sources and how they complement your personal savings and investments.

Creating a Retirement Savings Strategy

The heart of your retirement plan lies in your savings strategy. This strategy includes:

- Determining the Amount Needed: Calculate the amount required for a comfortable retirement based on your lifestyle goals and expected expenses. This includes considerations for housing, healthcare, leisure activities, and potential travel.
- Saving Consistently: Consistency is key. Regular contributions to retirement accounts, such as 401(k)s, IRAs, and other investment vehicles, ensure steady wealth accumulation.
- Diversifying Investments: Diversification within your retirement portfolio is vital. A mix of stocks, bonds, and other investment assets helps manage risk and optimize returns.
- Adjusting for Inflation: Account for the eroding effects of inflation over time by adjusting your retirement savings goals to maintain your purchasing power.

Understanding Retirement Accounts

Familiarize yourself with various retirement accounts, such as:

- 401(k)s: Commonly offered by employers, these tax-advantaged accounts allow contributions directly from your paycheck, often with employer matching.

- IRAs (Individual Retirement Accounts): These accounts offer tax advantages for individual retirement savings. Traditional IRAs provide tax-deferred growth, while Roth IRAs offer tax-free withdrawals in retirement.
- Other Investment Accounts: Explore brokerage accounts, annuities, and other investment vehicles as potential additions to your retirement savings strategy.

Strategies for Catching Up on Retirement Savings

For those who may have started their retirement planning later in life or have experienced setbacks, various strategies can help accelerate wealth accumulation. These include making catch-up contributions to retirement accounts, reevaluating investment allocations, and considering additional income streams.

Contingency Planning

While retirement planning focuses on the ideal retirement scenario, it's also crucial to incorporate contingency plans. These plans should address unexpected events such as health issues, unexpected expenses, or changes in financial circumstances. Adequate insurance coverage and an emergency fund are essential components of a robust contingency plan.

Estate Planning and Wealth Transfer

As retirement approaches, estate planning becomes increasingly significant. This involves creating a will, establishing trusts, and making decisions regarding the transfer of your wealth to beneficiaries. Effective estate planning ensures that your assets are distributed according to your wishes, minimizes tax implications, and provides financial security to your loved ones.

Enjoying Retirement

Retirement planning isn't solely about the accumulation of wealth. It's about creating a blueprint for a fulfilling retirement lifestyle. This includes considerations for where you'll live, how you'll spend your time, and how you'll maintain your physical and mental well-being.

Case Study - Mark's Retirement Journey

To provide a real-world perspective, a case study featuring Mark's retirement journey illustrates the practical application of retirement planning principles. By delving into Mark's experiences, we gain insights into the challenges and successes encountered on the path to retirement.

Retirement Lifestyle Considerations

Your retirement lifestyle should align with your values and aspirations. Factors to contemplate include:

- Housing: Decide whether to stay in your current home, downsize, or explore retirement communities.

- Hobbies and Interests: Identify activities that will bring you joy and purpose during retirement.
- Travel and Leisure: Plan how you'll spend your leisure time, which may include travel, pursuing hobbies, or engaging in volunteer work.

The Evolving Nature of Retirement

Retirement is no longer a one-size-fits-all concept. It has evolved into a dynamic phase of life with diverse options and opportunities. Understanding these changes and adapting your retirement plan accordingly is essential for a successful retirement journey.

Estate Planning and Wealth Transfer

Estate planning, an often overlooked facet of personal finance, takes center stage in this chapter. It's the art of orchestrating the management and transfer of your assets, both during your lifetime and after you pass away. A well-executed estate plan not only ensures the orderly distribution of your assets but also serves to minimize tax burdens and provide a secure financial future for your loved ones.

The Essence of Estate Planning

Estate planning is a multifaceted process that requires thoughtful consideration of how your assets will be managed, preserved, and ultimately distributed. It's not just for the wealthy; estate planning is an essential endeavor for anyone seeking to safeguard their assets, ensure their wishes are carried out, and provide for the well-being of their family.

Key Components of an Estate Plan

A comprehensive estate plan comprises several pivotal components, each serving a specific purpose in the seamless transition of your estate:

Will: A will is a legal document that outlines your preferences for the distribution of your assets after your demise. It also designates an executor to manage your estate, identifies beneficiaries, and delineates how your assets should be divided.

Trusts: Trusts are versatile legal entities designed to hold and manage assets on behalf of beneficiaries. They can streamline the probate process, provide specific instructions for asset distribution, and serve various purposes, from asset protection to tax planning.

Power of Attorney: A power of attorney grants a trusted individual the authority to handle your financial and legal matters if you become incapacitated.

Healthcare Proxy: A healthcare proxy designates someone to make medical decisions on your behalf in case you are unable to do so.

Living Will: A living will expresses your preferences regarding medical treatment and end-of-life decisions.

Beneficiary Designations: Designate beneficiaries for assets such as retirement accounts, life insurance policies, and investment accounts. These assets typically pass directly to beneficiaries and are not governed by your will.

Letter of Intent: While not legally binding, a letter of intent provides valuable guidance to your loved ones regarding personal and financial matters.

The Significance of a Will

A will often serves as the linchpin of an estate plan, accomplishing several critical objectives:

Asset Distribution: It delineates how your assets should be distributed, ensuring your wishes are honored.

Executor Appointment: You can appoint an executor to manage your estate, facilitating the smooth administration of your affairs.

Guardianship for Minors: If you have minor children, your will can designate guardians to care for them should you pass away.

Asset Protection: Your will can include provisions for protecting assets, such as creating trusts for beneficiaries.

Trusts in Estate Planning

Trusts are powerful tools in estate planning, capable of fulfilling a range of objectives:

Revocable Living Trust: This trust allows assets to bypass probate, ensuring a more efficient transition of assets to beneficiaries.

Irrevocable Trust: This type of trust may provide tax benefits and asset protection but typically cannot be altered once established.

Special Needs Trust: This trust is designed to provide for individuals with disabilities, preserving government benefits while offering additional support.

Estate Taxes and Mitigation Strategies

Estate taxes, often dubbed the "death tax," can apply to larger estates. Effective estate planning can help mitigate these tax burdens. Strategies may encompass gifting assets, setting up trusts, and making use of the annual gift tax exclusion.

Ongoing Review and Updates

Estate planning is not a one-and-done task; it should evolve in tandem with your life circumstances and changing laws. Regularly review and update your estate plan, especially after significant life events such as marriage, the birth of children, divorce, or the acquisition of substantial assets.

Case Study - The Anderson Family

To provide a real-world perspective on estate planning, we delve into the estate planning journey of the Anderson family. Their experiences and decisions offer insights into the complexities and considerations involved in crafting an effective estate plan.

Charitable Giving

Estate planning also provides opportunities for philanthropy. Charitable giving can be an integral part of your estate plan, allowing you to support causes you are passionate about and leave a lasting legacy.

Estate Planning Challenges

Estate planning can present complex challenges, such as family dynamics, diverse assets, or tax complexities. Seeking professional guidance from estate planning attorneys and financial advisors can be invaluable in navigating these challenges and crafting a plan that addresses your unique circumstances.

The Legacy of Your Estate Plan

In essence, estate planning is about creating a legacy. It ensures that your assets are distributed in alignment with your values and that your loved ones are provided for. Estate planning is a testament to your foresight, compassion, and commitment to securing the financial future of those you care about.

Achieving Financial Wellness

In the intricate landscape of personal finance, achieving financial wellness emerges as the ultimate objective. This chapter delves into the multifaceted realm of financial wellness, exploring the profound significance it holds in transforming your financial life. Financial wellness is more than just the absence of financial stress; it's a state of equilibrium where your financial resources align with your values, goals, and aspirations. It's a holistic approach to money management that extends beyond budgeting and investing, encompassing physical well-being, emotional health, and overall life satisfaction.

The Holistic Nature of Financial Wellness
Financial wellness is not a one-dimensional concept. It comprises several interconnected components, each influencing the others:

Financial Fitness: This dimension encompasses your financial knowledge and skills. It includes your ability to manage money effectively, create budgets, invest wisely, and make informed financial decisions.

Emotional Well-being: Your emotional health plays a vital role in financial wellness. Emotional well-being involves managing stress, anxiety, and emotions related to money. It's about developing a healthy relationship with money and reducing financial stress.

Physical Health: Physical health is intrinsically tied to financial wellness. Maintaining good health is an essential part of the financial wellness equation. Medical expenses and the impact of health on your ability to work can significantly affect your financial situation.

Social and Relationship Health: Healthy relationships and a strong support network can positively impact your financial wellness. Open communication about financial matters with your loved ones can lead to better financial outcomes.

Career Satisfaction: Your career and job satisfaction are closely linked to financial wellness. A fulfilling and stable career can lead to financial security and overall life satisfaction.

Life Satisfaction and Fulfillment: At the core of financial wellness is your overall life satisfaction and fulfillment. It's about aligning your financial resources with your values, goals, and aspirations, leading to a sense of purpose and contentment.

Setting Financial Goals

Financial wellness begins with setting clear, realistic financial goals. Your goals give you a purpose and direction for your financial journey. These goals can encompass various aspects of your life, from saving for retirement and buying a home to funding education and pursuing travel dreams.

Budgeting and Financial Planning

A budget serves as a roadmap to your financial goals. It's a tool that helps you track income and expenses, ensuring that you live within your means and allocate funds to your priorities. Effective financial planning goes beyond budgeting and encompasses goal-setting, emergency funds, and debt management.

Managing Debt

Managing debt is an integral component of financial wellness. It involves understanding different types of debt, creating a debt repayment plan, and avoiding new debt while focusing on paying off existing debt.

Saving and Investing

Saving and investing are key to building financial security and achieving long-term goals. It involves building an emergency fund, understanding the power of compound interest, and creating a diversified investment portfolio.

Risk Management

Risk management includes safeguarding your financial well-being through insurance. Health, life, auto, and home insurance can protect you and your assets from unexpected events.

Financial Literacy and Education

Financial wellness is closely linked to financial literacy. Continuously improving your financial knowledge and skills is an essential part of financial wellness. It empowers you to make informed decisions, navigate complex financial products, and adapt to changing financial landscapes.

Emergency Funds and Contingency Planning

Preparing for unexpected expenses through emergency funds is essential. Having a financial safety net helps you navigate unforeseen financial challenges without compromising your long-term financial goals.

Retirement Planning

Retirement planning is a critical aspect of financial wellness. It involves setting clear retirement goals, assessing your current financial position, and creating a retirement savings strategy. Effective retirement planning ensures that you can enjoy your golden years without financial stress.

Charitable Giving

Financial wellness includes the opportunity to give back. Charitable giving allows you to support causes you are passionate about, creating a sense of purpose and contributing to the well-being of society.

The Role of Financial Advisors

Financial advisors play a significant role in achieving financial wellness. They provide guidance on investment strategies, retirement planning, estate planning, and other financial aspects. Their expertise can help you make informed decisions and navigate complex financial matters.

Financial Wellness Challenges

Financial wellness is not without its challenges. Economic fluctuations, unexpected expenses, and life events can impact your financial well-being. Staying flexible and adaptable in your financial approach is essential in overcoming these challenges.

Case Study - The Johnsons' Journey to Financial Wellness

The Johnsons' story provides a real-life perspective on achieving financial wellness. Their experiences and financial journey illustrate the challenges and successes encountered while pursuing a state of financial equilibrium.

Financial Wellness and Life Satisfaction

In conclusion, financial wellness is a dynamic and multi-faceted concept that extends beyond mere money management. It's about aligning your financial resources with your values and goals while maintaining emotional and physical well-being. Financial wellness contributes to overall life satisfaction, providing you with the means to pursue your dreams, secure your future, and enjoy a fulfilling and purposeful life.

Investment Strategies for Wealth Accumulation

In the intricate realm of personal finance, investment strategies serve as the engine that powers wealth accumulation and financial growth. This chapter delves into the multifaceted world of investments, exploring the myriad strategies and principles that enable you to make informed decisions, optimize returns, and achieve your long-term financial goals. Investment strategies are not one-size-fits-all; they encompass a spectrum of choices, each tailored to individual preferences, risk tolerance, and financial objectives.

Understanding Investment Basics

Investing is the act of allocating your financial resources, such as money and assets, with the expectation of generating a return or profit over time. The core concept underlying all investments is the potential to grow your wealth by putting your money to work for you. Here are key principles to grasp when understanding investment basics:

Risk and Return: A fundamental tenet of investing is the risk-return trade-off. Generally, investments that carry higher risk have the potential for greater returns, while lower-risk investments typically yield more modest returns. The key is to find the right balance that aligns with your financial goals and risk tolerance.

Diversification: Diversification involves spreading your investments across various asset classes, sectors, and geographical regions. This strategy mitigates risk by reducing your exposure to any single investment. Diversification can be achieved through various investment vehicles, including stocks, bonds, real estate, and more.

Time Horizon: Your investment time horizon is the period over which you intend to hold your investments. It is a crucial factor that influences your investment strategy. Short-term goals may require conservative, low-risk investments, while long-term objectives can accommodate higher-risk, potentially higher-reward investments.

Asset Allocation: Asset allocation is the process of determining how to distribute your investments among different asset classes, such as stocks, bonds, and cash. Your asset allocation should align with your financial goals, risk tolerance, and investment time horizon.

Active vs. Passive Investing: Active investing involves frequent buying and selling of investments in an attempt to outperform the market. Passive investing, on the other hand, seeks to match the performance of a market index or benchmark. Both approaches have their merits and drawbacks, and the choice depends on your investment philosophy and preferences.

Investment Vehicles and Options

A vast array of investment vehicles and options is available to investors. These include:

Stocks: Stocks represent ownership in a company and provide the potential for capital appreciation through price increases and dividends.

Bonds: Bonds are debt securities that pay periodic interest and return the principal amount at maturity. They are typically less risky than stocks and offer predictable income.

Mutual Funds: Mutual funds pool money from multiple investors to invest in a diversified portfolio of stocks, bonds, or other securities. They provide diversification and professional management.

Exchange-Traded Funds (ETFs): ETFs are similar to mutual funds but trade like individual stocks on stock exchanges. They offer diversification and are known for low expenses.

Real Estate: Real estate investments involve owning properties or investing in real estate investment trusts (REITs). Real estate can provide rental income and potential property appreciation.

Retirement Accounts: Retirement accounts like 401(k)s and IRAs offer tax advantages for long-term retirement savings.

Alternative Investments: Alternative investments encompass assets such as commodities, hedge funds, private equity, and more. They can be used to diversify a portfolio but often come with higher risk.

Investment Strategies

Investment strategies vary widely and should align with your financial goals, risk tolerance, and investment time horizon. Here are some common investment strategies to consider:

Buy and Hold: Buy and hold is a long-term investment strategy where you purchase assets and hold onto them for an extended period, typically with the expectation of capital appreciation.

Value Investing: Value investing involves selecting assets that are considered undervalued and trading below their intrinsic value. The goal is to benefit from their potential for price appreciation.

Growth Investing: Growth investing focuses on assets with strong growth potential, often in emerging industries or sectors. The strategy aims to capitalize on the expected growth of these assets.

Income Investing: Income investing emphasizes investments that provide regular income, such as dividend-paying stocks or interest-bearing bonds.

Dollar-Cost Averaging: Dollar-cost averaging involves investing a fixed amount of money at regular intervals, regardless of the asset's price. This strategy can reduce the impact of market volatility.

Market Timing: Market timing is an active strategy where investors attempt to buy assets at the lowest prices and sell at the highest. It requires predicting market movements and can be challenging.

Risk Management: Risk management strategies focus on preserving capital and minimizing potential losses. These strategies often involve diversification, asset allocation, and risk-reducing techniques.

Robo-Advisors and Financial Advisors

Robo-advisors are automated investment platforms that use algorithms to create and manage diversified portfolios based on your risk tolerance and financial goals. Financial advisors, on the other hand, provide personalized investment advice and portfolio management based on your individual circumstances.

The Importance of Monitoring and Review

Investing is not a set-and-forget activity. Regularly monitoring and reviewing your investments is crucial to ensure they remain aligned with your goals and risk tolerance. Adjustments may be needed as your circumstances change.

Investing for the Long Term

Investing is a long-term endeavor. It's important to resist the temptation of making impulsive decisions based on short-term market fluctuations. Staying committed to your long-term investment strategy is often the key to success.

Case Study - Emily's Investment Journey

To provide real-world insights into investment strategies, we explore Emily's investment journey. Her experiences and decisions offer valuable lessons and practical examples of how investment strategies can be applied in real life.

Achieving Financial Goals through Investment

In summary, investment strategies are a vital component of wealth accumulation and achieving financial goals. Whether you seek to fund your children's education, buy a home, or secure a comfortable retirement, selecting the right investment strategy and vehicle is paramount. By understanding the principles of investing and tailoring your strategy to your unique circumstances, you can pave the way for a more prosperous financial future.

Navigating Tax-Efficient Financial Planning

In the intricate world of personal finance, the impact of taxes on your financial well-being is profound. This chapter explores the multifaceted realm of tax-efficient financial planning, which is instrumental in optimizing your financial outcomes, reducing tax liabilities, and achieving your long-term financial objectives. Understanding the tax implications of your financial decisions and structuring your financial plan to minimize tax burdens is a fundamental aspect of prudent financial management.

The Role of Taxes in Financial Planning

Taxes are a constant companion in financial planning. They can significantly affect your wealth accumulation, investment returns, and overall financial security. Effective tax planning is about making informed decisions that minimize your tax liabilities while ensuring compliance with tax laws.

Understanding the Tax System

Understanding the tax system is the cornerstone of tax-efficient financial planning. Key aspects include:

Tax Brackets: Tax rates are tiered, with higher income levels subject to higher tax rates. Knowing your tax bracket allows you to make informed decisions about income and deductions.

Tax Deductions: Tax deductions reduce your taxable income and, consequently, your tax liability. Common deductions include mortgage interest, medical expenses, and charitable contributions.

Tax Credits: Tax credits directly reduce your tax liability, providing a dollar-for-dollar reduction in the taxes you owe. Examples include the Child Tax Credit and the Earned Income Tax Credit.

Capital Gains Tax: Capital gains tax is assessed on the profits from the sale of assets such as stocks, real estate, and investments. Understanding the tax implications of capital gains is vital in investment planning.

Estate Taxes: Estate taxes can affect the transfer of wealth to heirs and beneficiaries. Estate planning strategies aim to minimize the impact of estate taxes.

Tax-Efficient Investment Strategies

Investing with tax efficiency in mind is essential for maximizing returns. Strategies include:

Tax-Advantaged Accounts: Utilize tax-advantaged accounts such as 401(k)s, IRAs, and HSAs to benefit from tax deductions, tax-deferred growth, or tax-free withdrawals.

Tax-Loss Harvesting: Offset capital gains with capital losses to minimize your tax liability. This strategy involves selling investments at a loss to reduce your overall taxable gains.

Long-Term Capital Gains: Holding investments for over a year can qualify you for lower long-term capital gains tax rates.

Municipal Bonds: Municipal bonds often offer tax-free interest income, making them a tax-efficient investment for high-income individuals.

Roth Conversions: Converting traditional retirement accounts to Roth IRAs can provide tax-free withdrawals in retirement. This strategy may involve paying taxes upfront but can be advantageous in the long run.

Asset Location: Allocate investments strategically between tax-advantaged and taxable accounts to maximize tax efficiency. Tax-efficient investments, such as index funds, can be held in taxable accounts.

Charitable Giving: Donating appreciated assets to charities can provide a double benefit—supporting a cause you care about while avoiding capital gains tax.

Business Owners and Self-Employed Individuals
Business owners and self-employed individuals have unique tax considerations. Strategies include:

Business Deductions: Identify business-related expenses that can be deducted to reduce taxable income.

Retirement Plans: Establish retirement plans for yourself and employees to benefit from tax advantages and save for retirement.

Tax Credits: Explore tax credits available to businesses, such as the Small Business Health Care Tax Credit.

Hiring and Compensation Strategies: Consider hiring and compensation strategies that align with tax incentives, such as the Work Opportunity Tax Credit.

Advanced Tax Planning Strategies

Advanced tax planning strategies are tailored to individuals with complex financial situations. These strategies may involve trusts, gifting, and estate planning to minimize tax implications.

The Role of Tax Professionals

Tax professionals, including certified public accountants (CPAs) and tax attorneys, play a pivotal role in tax-efficient financial planning. Their expertise can help you navigate complex tax laws, maximize deductions, and develop advanced strategies.

Case Study - The Lewis Family's Tax-Efficient Journey

To illustrate the practical application of tax-efficient financial planning, we explore the Lewis family's financial journey. Their experiences and decisions provide real-world insights into how tax-efficient strategies can be employed to optimize financial outcomes.

The Future of Tax-Efficient Financial Planning
Tax laws and regulations are subject to change. Staying informed about tax developments and adapting your financial plan to align with current tax codes is vital for continued tax efficiency.

The Intersection of Financial Goals and Tax Efficiency
Tax-efficient financial planning is a dynamic and integral aspect of personal finance. By integrating tax considerations into your financial decisions and utilizing tax-efficient strategies, you can maximize your financial resources, reduce tax liabilities, and achieve your long-term financial goals. Tax efficiency is not about evading taxes but about optimizing your financial well-being within the bounds of the law.

Protecting Your Financial Legacy

In the complex tapestry of personal finance, protecting your financial legacy emerges as a paramount consideration. This chapter delves into the multifaceted world of legacy planning, offering insights into the strategies and principles that help safeguard your wealth, ensure its orderly distribution, and leave a lasting impact on the generations to come. Legacy planning is about more than just the allocation of assets; it encompasses a comprehensive approach to preserving your values, wisdom, and financial security for your heirs and beneficiaries.

The Essence of Legacy Planning

Legacy planning extends far beyond the mere distribution of assets. It involves the deliberate consideration of how you want to be remembered and the impact you wish to leave on your loved ones, your community, and the world. At its core, legacy planning is about safeguarding your financial resources and creating a lasting testament to your values and aspirations.

Components of Legacy Planning

Legacy planning encompasses various key components:

Wills and Trusts: A will is a foundational document that outlines your preferences for the distribution of your assets. Trusts, on the other hand, provide additional layers of control and can help minimize the probate process.

Power of Attorney and Healthcare Directives: These legal documents grant someone you trust the authority to manage your financial and healthcare affairs in case you become incapacitated.

Beneficiary Designations: Designate beneficiaries for assets such as life insurance policies, retirement accounts, and investment accounts. These assets typically pass directly to beneficiaries and are not governed by your will.

Charitable Giving: Legacy planning often includes charitable giving, allowing you to support causes you are passionate about and leave a philanthropic legacy.

Estate Taxes and Strategies: Effective legacy planning may involve strategies to mitigate estate taxes and maximize the transfer of wealth to your heirs.

Business Succession Planning: If you own a business, business succession planning is a critical component of legacy planning. It involves identifying successors and ensuring the seamless transition of your business.

Digital Legacy: In the digital age, it's important to consider your digital legacy. This involves instructions for the management of your online accounts, digital assets, and social media presence.

Family Communication and Education: Open and transparent communication with your family about your financial plans and intentions can help prevent disputes and misunderstandings. Additionally, providing financial education to heirs can equip them with the knowledge to manage their inheritance responsibly.

The Role of Legacy Advisors

Legacy advisors, including estate planning attorneys, financial advisors, and tax professionals, play a crucial role in legacy planning. Their expertise can help you navigate complex legal and financial matters, ensuring your legacy planning aligns with your goals and complies with relevant laws.

Case Study - The Reynolds Family's Legacy Journey

To provide real-world insights into legacy planning, we explore the Reynolds family's legacy journey. Their experiences and decisions offer valuable lessons and practical examples of how legacy planning can be applied in real life.

Maintaining and Updating Your Legacy Plan

Legacy planning is not a one-time task; it should evolve with your life circumstances and changing laws. Regularly reviewing and updating your legacy plan, especially after significant life events, is essential in ensuring it remains aligned with your intentions.

The Legacy of Your Legacy

In essence, legacy planning is about creating a lasting impact that extends beyond your lifetime. It ensures that your financial resources are distributed in alignment with your values and goals, and that your loved ones are provided for. Your legacy is a testament to your foresight, compassion, and commitment to securing the financial future of those you care about.

Conclusion: The Ongoing Journey

As our exploration of personal finance draws to a close, legacy planning serves as the culminating chapter in this comprehensive journey. Legacy planning is the legacy of a journey marked by financial wisdom, prudent decisions, and a vision for a secure and impactful future. Whether you aim to provide for your heirs, support charitable causes, or leave a profound mark on the world, legacy planning is the final brushstroke on the canvas of your financial life.

Achieving Financial Independence and Freedom

In the intricate tapestry of personal finance, the pursuit of financial independence and freedom stands as the ultimate aspiration. This chapter embarks on a journey to explore the multifaceted world of financial independence, offering insights into the principles, strategies, and mindset needed to break free from the constraints of financial dependence and embrace a life of autonomy and choice.

Defining Financial Independence

Financial independence, often referred to as "FI," is a state where you have amassed sufficient financial resources to cover your living expenses and sustain your desired lifestyle without the need for traditional employment or a paycheck. It signifies a transition from being reliant on earned income to a position where your investments, assets, and passive income streams provide for your financial needs.

The Importance of Financial Independence

Achieving financial independence offers numerous benefits:

Freedom and Autonomy: Financial independence grants you the freedom to make choices based on your preferences and values. It liberates you from the necessity of working solely for a paycheck.

Reduced Stress: Freedom from financial worries and the security of knowing that you can sustain your lifestyle can significantly reduce stress and enhance overall well-being.

Pursuit of Passion: Financial independence enables you to pursue your passions and interests without being bound by the need to earn a living.

Work as a Choice: You have the option to work or engage in activities that fulfill you, rather than feeling compelled to work for financial survival.

Early Retirement: Financial independence often aligns with early retirement or achieving retirement at a younger age, providing more years of leisure and self-discovery.

Pathways to Financial Independence

The journey to financial independence involves several key pathways:

Income and Savings: Growing your income and savings rate is a fundamental step toward financial independence. You can achieve this through salary increases, career advancements, and a disciplined approach to saving and budgeting.

Investing: Investing your savings wisely is crucial to building wealth and creating a source of passive income. This involves strategic asset allocation, diversification, and a long-term perspective.

Debt Management: Managing and reducing debt, especially high-interest debt, is essential. Being debt-free or having manageable debt levels can expedite your path to financial independence.

Passive Income: Developing passive income streams, such as rental income, dividends, interest, or royalties, can accelerate your journey toward financial independence.

Retirement Accounts: Taking full advantage of retirement accounts, like 401(k)s and IRAs, can provide tax advantages and accelerate your retirement savings.

Side Hustles and Entrepreneurship: Side businesses or entrepreneurial endeavors can augment your income and create new income sources that contribute to financial independence.

Mindset and Lifestyle Choices

The path to financial independence is not solely a numbers game; it also involves mindset and lifestyle choices:

Frugality: Living below your means and practicing frugality can increase your savings rate and expedite your journey to financial independence.

Simplicity: Simplifying your life and reducing unnecessary expenses can free up resources to invest and save.

Delayed Gratification: Being patient and willing to delay immediate gratification in favor of long-term financial goals is a hallmark of those on the path to financial independence.

Self-Education: Continuously educating yourself about personal finance, investments, and income opportunities is essential. Knowledge is a powerful tool on the journey to financial independence.

Community and Support: Joining or creating a community of like-minded individuals pursuing financial independence can provide support, accountability, and shared experiences.

Redefining Retirement

Financial independence often leads to a redefinition of retirement. It's no longer solely about ceasing work but about having the choice to work on your own terms. Retirement can involve new adventures, personal projects, volunteering, or pursuing a lifelong dream.

Challenges and Considerations

While the pursuit of financial independence is rewarding, it is not without challenges:

Sacrifice: Achieving financial independence may require temporary sacrifices in terms of lifestyle, expenses, and discretionary spending.

Market Volatility: Investment markets can be volatile, impacting the growth of your portfolio. A well-structured investment strategy can mitigate this risk.

Healthcare: Healthcare costs in retirement can be a significant consideration. Planning for healthcare expenses is a vital part of the financial independence journey.

Inflation: Inflation erodes the purchasing power of your savings over time. It's crucial to invest in assets that outpace inflation.

Taxes: Managing tax liabilities in retirement and while pursuing financial independence is vital to preserving your wealth.

Balancing Life Enjoyment: Striking a balance between pursuing financial independence and enjoying life along the way is essential. Overemphasizing future goals at the expense of present happiness may not be the most fulfilling path.

Conclusion: The Journey to Financial Independence

As our exploration of personal finance nears its end, the pursuit of financial independence stands as the grand finale. Achieving financial independence is a transformative journey, marked by disciplined financial management, strategic investments, and a shift in mindset. It is a path that leads to freedom, autonomy, and the realization of your dreams.

The Ever-Evolving Landscape of Personal Finance

In the intricate tapestry of personal finance, the only constant is change. This final chapter of our exploration delves into the ever-evolving landscape of personal finance, emphasizing the importance of adaptability, continuous learning, and financial agility in the face of evolving economic conditions, societal shifts, and technological advancements. Understanding that personal finance is a dynamic, ever-changing field is essential to secure your financial well-being and thrive in an unpredictable world.

The Unpredictable Nature of Finance

Financial markets and economic conditions are subject to constant change. Market fluctuations, economic cycles, political events, and global crises can have a profound impact on your financial situation. Recognizing that financial stability is not guaranteed, you must develop strategies to adapt to change.

Financial Resilience

Financial resilience is the ability to withstand and recover from financial setbacks. Building financial resilience involves:

Emergency Funds: Maintaining a sufficient emergency fund to cover unexpected expenses and disruptions in income.

Debt Management: Managing and reducing debt to minimize financial vulnerabilities.

Insurance: Adequate insurance coverage, including health, life, auto, and home insurance, can protect against unforeseen events.

Diversification: Diversifying investments across different asset classes and regions to mitigate risk.

Planning for Retirement

Retirement planning remains a critical aspect of personal finance. However, the landscape of retirement is changing:

Retirement Age: The traditional retirement age is evolving. Some individuals choose to work longer, while others opt for early retirement or phased retirement.

Longevity: Longer life expectancy requires more extended financial planning to ensure retirement funds last through a more extended retirement period.

Retirement Savings Vehicles: Retirement account rules and regulations may change, impacting your retirement savings strategies. Staying informed about these changes is crucial.

Advanced Investment Strategies

Incorporating advanced investment strategies can enhance financial security:

Tax-Efficient Investing: Maximizing tax advantages and optimizing investment returns through tax-efficient strategies remains a vital component of personal finance.

Passive vs. Active Investing: Understanding the benefits and drawbacks of passive and active investing can help you make informed decisions.

Impact Investing: Impact investing, which combines financial returns with a commitment to social or environmental causes, is gaining popularity as people seek to align their investments with their values.

Real Estate and Alternative Investments: Exploring opportunities in real estate and alternative investments can diversify your portfolio and provide income streams.

Legacy and Estate Planning

The legacy you leave and how you structure your estate may continue to evolve:

Estate Tax Laws: Changes in estate tax laws can impact your estate planning strategies.

Digital Estate Planning: The management of digital assets, online accounts, and digital legacies is a growing consideration in estate planning.

Charitable Giving: Charitable giving can play an integral role in legacy planning, allowing you to support causes you are passionate about.

Healthcare and Medical Costs

As healthcare costs continue to rise, planning for medical expenses in retirement becomes increasingly important. Medicare, supplemental insurance, and long-term care considerations are crucial components of financial planning.

Technological Advancements

The digital age has transformed personal finance:

Fintech: Financial technology, or fintech, is revolutionizing how people manage their money, offering tools for budgeting, investing, and financial education.

Cybersecurity: Protecting your financial data and identity is paramount in an era of increased digital threats.

Cryptocurrency: Cryptocurrencies have emerged as a new asset class, with the potential to impact investment portfolios and financial transactions.

Continuous Learning

Continuously improving your financial knowledge and skills is essential:

Financial Literacy: Regularly updating your financial literacy equips you to make informed decisions, navigate complex financial products, and adapt to changing financial landscapes.

Professional Advice: Consult financial professionals, including financial advisors, tax experts, and estate planning attorneys, for guidance on complex financial matters.

The Evolving Nature of Work

The nature of work is changing with the rise of the gig economy, remote work, and automation. Understanding the impact of these shifts on income, taxes, and retirement planning is critical.

The Ongoing Journey

In conclusion, the ever-evolving landscape of personal finance requires a commitment to adaptability, lifelong learning, and financial agility. As you navigate the unpredictable financial terrain, you have the opportunity to secure your financial well-being and thrive in a world of constant change.

A Holistic Approach to Wealth and Well-Being

In the intricate tapestry of personal finance, true prosperity extends beyond financial numbers and spreadsheets. This final chapter of our exploration embarks on a journey to explore a holistic approach to wealth and well-being, emphasizing the interconnectedness of financial health with physical, mental, and emotional well-being. It's a reminder that achieving wealth, financial independence, and a secure legacy is ultimately about enhancing the quality of life, fostering meaningful relationships, and nurturing a sense of purpose and fulfillment.

The Intersection of Wealth and Well-Being

Wealth and well-being are intertwined in a delicate dance, each influencing and supporting the other. A holistic approach to prosperity acknowledges that true wealth encompasses more than monetary riches. It encompasses physical vitality, mental clarity, emotional resilience, and a deep sense of fulfillment.

Physical Well-Being

Physical health is the foundation of overall well-being. A few key considerations include:

Nutrition: A balanced and nourishing diet provides the energy and vitality needed to pursue financial goals and lead a fulfilling life.

Exercise: Regular physical activity enhances physical health, reduces stress, and boosts cognitive function.

Sleep: Quality sleep is essential for mental clarity, emotional balance, and physical recovery.

Preventive Healthcare: Regular medical check-ups and preventive healthcare measures can catch issues early and reduce long-term medical costs.

Mental and Emotional Well-Being

A sound mind and emotional resilience are essential components of holistic well-being:

Mental Health: Recognizing the importance of mental health and seeking support when needed is crucial.

Stress Management: Learning to manage stress through mindfulness, relaxation techniques, and a work-life balance can enhance overall well-being.

Social Connections: Nurturing meaningful relationships and social connections contributes to emotional well-being.

Purpose and Fulfillment

A sense of purpose and fulfillment transcends material wealth:

Lifelong Learning: Pursuing continuous education and personal growth enhances not only financial knowledge but also mental well-being.

Community Engagement: Engaging in community service or philanthropic endeavors can provide a sense of purpose and fulfillment.

Work-Life Balance: Balancing professional and personal life is instrumental in maintaining overall well-being.

Gratitude and Mindfulness: Practicing gratitude and mindfulness fosters emotional and mental well-being and enhances life satisfaction.

Legacy and Values

Legacy and values are integral to a holistic approach to wealth:

Teaching Financial Literacy: Passing on financial knowledge to future generations is a meaningful legacy.

Generosity: Incorporating charitable giving and supporting causes you believe in as part of your legacy can leave a profound impact.

Living Your Values: Aligning your financial decisions with your core values ensures a life lived with integrity and authenticity.

The Pursuit of Holistic Prosperity

Holistic prosperity is about fostering a harmonious and balanced life. It involves being mindful of how financial choices impact not just your bank account but your overall well-being.

Financial Independence and Freedom

Financial independence remains a significant milestone in holistic prosperity:

Work as a Choice: Achieving financial independence grants you the freedom to work as a choice, not a necessity.

Legacy and Impact: Financial independence provides the means to leave a legacy and make a meaningful impact on the world.

Financial Education and Empowerment

Financial education is a crucial aspect of holistic well-being:

Empowerment: Being financially literate empowers you to make informed choices, minimize financial stress, and navigate life's financial challenges.

Continuous Learning: Embracing a growth mindset and a commitment to lifelong learning ensures you stay informed about changing financial landscapes.

The Ongoing Journey of Prosperity

The pursuit of a holistic approach to wealth and well-being is the culmination of our exploration of personal finance. It underscores that wealth is not merely about amassing money; it's about enriching your life with vitality, purpose, and fulfillment.

Reflections and the Ever-Expanding Horizon of Personal Finance

In this concluding chapter of our extensive odyssey through the realm of personal finance, it is an opportune juncture to pause, introspect, and cast our gaze towards the future. Personal finance is not a static destination but an ever-evolving expedition, an ongoing narrative that requires continuous learning, adaptation, and engagement. Here, we explore the significance of reflection in our financial journey, celebrate the knowledge amassed, and contemplate the future of personal finance, all within the context of your pivotal role in shaping its course.

Harnessing the Power of Reflection

Reflecting on your personal finance journey wields an incredible potential for personal growth and improvement:

Assessment: Take a deliberate pause to assess your financial voyage, cataloging your progress, accomplishments, and evolving objectives. This moment of reflection is an opportunity to commend your achievements and candidly recognize areas demanding further attention and enhancement.

Extracting Insights and Wisdom: Delve into the treasury of lessons you've gleaned through your financial experiences. Explore the insights accrued through both successes and challenges, pondering how they've molded your financial sagacity.

Triumph Over Adversities: Acknowledge the adversities and obstacles surmounted on your financial journey. Recognize the tenacity and determination that have propelled you to your current vantage point.

Gratitude as a Beacon: Extend your reflections to express gratitude for the privileges and opportunities that have intersected your path. Be thankful for the knowledge you've accumulated, the resources at your disposal, and the horizons of possibility that unfold before you.

The Landscape of Future Personal Finance

Personal finance, like the flowing tides of the ocean, is ceaselessly evolving, subject to the influence of diverse forces and trends that shape its contours:

The Digital Revolution: Technology is rapidly permeating the personal finance arena, ushering in a new era of fintech solutions, digital currencies, and accessible online financial management tools. The digitization of financial processes is altering the way individuals manage and invest their wealth.

Environmental and Social Consciousness: A growing emphasis on ethical investing and sustainable finance is beginning to reconfigure the investment landscape. Investors are increasingly directing their resources towards endeavors that align with their social and environmental values, transcending the traditional focus on profits.

Inclusivity and Accessibility: There is a mounting endeavor to enhance access to financial services and knowledge, ensuring that financial inclusivity is not just a catchphrase but an actionable reality for all individuals, irrespective of their socio-economic backgrounds.

Changing Notions of Retirement: The very concept of retirement is undergoing a transformation. More people are embracing alternative retirement paths, with some opting for early retirement or adopting a phased approach to retirement. The pursuit of financial independence has taken center stage.

Education and Empowerment: Financial literacy and education are occupying an increasingly prominent position in societal discourse. The realization of the vital role of financial knowledge in personal empowerment is encouraging a new generation of informed and astute individuals to take the reins of their financial destinies.

Your Role in Shaping the Future

In this perpetually evolving landscape of personal finance, your role is both pivotal and transformative:

Lifelong Learning: Commit yourself to the never-ending pursuit of knowledge. Endeavor to remain in tune with the latest developments in financial strategies, products, and trends that have the potential to impact your financial journey.

Advocacy and Knowledge Dissemination: As a guardian of financial wisdom, you have the capacity to be an advocate for financial literacy and inclusivity. Extend your wisdom to others, sharing your experiences and insights to empower individuals who are setting out on their financial journey.

A Legacy of Impact: Reflect upon the legacy you aspire to leave, both in financial terms and as a repository of values. Your actions today can radiate across the canvas of the future, profoundly impacting not only the material well-being of generations to come but also the character and essence of the world they inhabit.

Balance and Well-Being: Finally, bear in mind that personal finance is not an end in itself; it is a conduit to a greater quality of life, one rich with health, contentment, and meaning. Ensure that your financial choices are in harmonious alignment with your overall well-being and life's aspirations.

The Unending Odyssey

In conclusion, we arrive at the terminus of our journey through the multifaceted world of personal finance. Yet, it is vital to acknowledge that the path of personal finance is not linear; it is an enduring expedition of growth, adaptation, and continual self-discovery. The knowledge you have acquired and the principles you have absorbed constitute the foundational bedrock upon which you will continue to construct and refine your financial destiny.

In Gratitude and Hope

As we bid adieu to this exploration, we do so with profound gratitude for your unwavering commitment and with unyielding hope for your forthcoming financial well-being. May your pursuit be crowned with financial prosperity, filled with enriching life experiences, and guided by a profound sense of purpose, wisdom, and abundance.

While your personal finance journey unfurls, keep in mind that you are not traversing this path in solitude. The world of personal finance extends as an expansive landscape, and you, equipped with your knowledge and insights, possess the acumen to navigate it skillfully. May the principles you have embraced serve as a guiding star on your voyage to financial accomplishment, well-being, fulfillment, and enduring prosperity.